# Pelmanism

## A Whole New Mind

### Change Your Brain, Change Your Life

## Pelman Institute of America

For information regarding special discounts for bulk purchases,

please contact BN Publishing

sales@bnpublishing.net

Cover Design: J. Neuman

**www.bnpublishing.net**

info@bnpublishing.net

# CONTENTS

## FOREWORD

Once more the aim before us is the development of *Personal Power*. This time it is the power to focus Attention. The first thing you have to do is to realize its importance. Probably you have already realized it; but, if not, remember this: that the vagaries of a wandering mind explain many of the failures of our modern life.

Resolve to be master of the thought process, not its slave. It is easy when you know how, and this Lesson will reveal to you the secret. Study it closely. Practice all the exercises. You will soon begin to feel a firmer mental grip. The feeling of futility and superficiality which has been oppressing you will soon leave you, because Attention permits you to acquire sound knowledge, and sound knowledge means new ideas. This applies equally to those engaged in business and professional pursuits.

# 1—MOVEMENT vs. FIXATION

It is erroneous to imagine that concentration means *fixation*; it means a controlled *movement*. This expression may seem contradictory; but let us explain. You sit down to solve a problem, any kind of problem. Difficult ones are plentiful, but we shall take a familiar one, because it serves our present purpose. Suppose it is the problem of building a garage somewhere on the lot. The idea in its persistent form occurred to you in the train: you saw a new garage being built, and all the vague, scattered wishes of the past culminated in one definite desire. You felt you must have a garage of your own. So you find a quiet spot, light your pipe, and begin to ponder the matter.

First, you have to decide whether you can afford the outlay. After some hurried calculations, you begin to see light. Now you become a little more critical. There is the cost of upkeep to consider; heat for the winter, repairs, painting, and so forth. When you have turned these and similar items over in your mind, you find you can decide the issue in the affirmative, and you proceed with the preliminary measures.

## THE CIRCLE OF RELATED IDEAS

Now what has happened in your mind during this exercise in concentrated effort? Let us say nothing about the ideas, hopes, desires, or doubts

which momentarily came into consciousness before you finally solved the problem; they are
not unimportant, but they are not our chief concern here. We are dealing principally with your
determination to fix your attention on the problem of building a garage until you had solved it
one way or the other; and if you are candid, you
will admit, on reflection, that you did not focus
your attention on the matter as rigidly as does,
for example, an astronomer on a star. You
shifted your attention from one aspect of the
subject to another, then back again to the start-
ing point, then to a new aspect altogether, until
you proved that concentration was not fixation
but controlled movement. Let us see if we can
make a diagram of it:

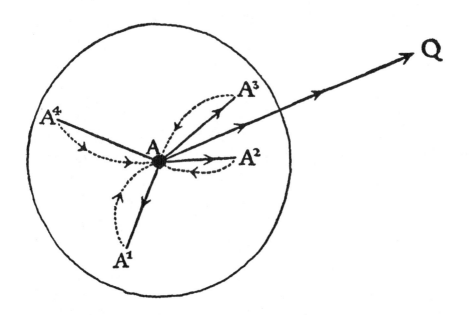

## CONCENTRATION AND CHANGE

In this figure the circle stands for the area in which the mind moves freely among the intimately related phases of the problem. A, the center of the circle, is the problem itself: a garage. To be or not to be? It is manifest you cannot solve anything by fixing your attention on the problem itself. If you make the attempt you simply become unpleasantly and increasingly aware of the fact that there *is* a problem.

Every problem is made up of parts, and each part in turn must receive attention. So you may wisely move from A to $A^1$, which deals with the cost of building. This means that for the time being you forget the garage altogether in order to discover how much money you can spare.

When you have ascertained this, you return immediately to A and almost instantaneously find yourself at $A^2$, the cost of upkeep. You remember that Rhodes, your friend in Yonkers, gave you a statement of his annual expenses in this matter, but you believe you can have your heating installed for less, and you also remember having seen a certain heater that was guaranteed to function efficiently at a considerably cheaper rate. Returning to the original item of cost, you add up the various items and conclude you are financially capable of projecting your plan for a garage. Back again at A you are switched off to $A^3$, then to $A^4$; we have not specified them all, but those we have examined are sufficient for our purpose.

## ATTENTION vs. MIND-WANDERING

We desired simply to demonstrate that to concentrate on a problem does not mean to study it as if one were hypnotized. It implies nothing more than a critical consideration of the various phases of the matter; and the whole process represents a mental operation in which the mind moves freely as it touches upon this phase and that. A man with good powers of attention can shift his attention from point to point and return at will to the original center. A man with poor abilities goes from A to A$^1$ like a flash. He pauses for a moment, then with lightning speed, is back to A. At this point, his attention wanders to distant matters: golf, his income-tax statement, a love affair, or anything at all. How do we explain this mind-wandering? The man who attends poorly lacks control of his mental processes; he is the slave of association, when he should be its master. One disconnected thought leads to another, and in a little while, this individual forgets what he was originally considering. We shall later on show by what means he may establish himself master.

## WHAT PSYCHOLOGISTS SAY

You have, perhaps, been taught to believe that concentration means fixing the attention on

something. Very well, let us ask two questions:
(a) what is the orthodox definition? and (b) is
it really possible to *fix* the attention exclusively
on any one thing? The first question is easily
answered, for all authorities are practically
unanimous in saying that attention, or concentration, cannot be *fixed* on anything; there must
be a change in the subject or object, in the mind
itself, or the thing looked at.

The object changes when you fix your attention on the cinema screen. The subject changes
when your mind perceives the various details of
the thing looked at. Let that thing be a book
lying on the table. The book itself does not
change, but the attention of your mind changes
as you gaze at it. Just try the experiment. You
will discover that although you concentrate on
the book, as such, your attention is caught by its
component parts: first, by its binding, its general
appearance, its weight, its title, and so on. These
characteristics serve to attract one's attention
which in the well-trained mind moves logically
from one feature to the next.

## SELF-HYPNOTISM

This explanation answers also the second
question. The act of fixing your attention on
one object would not be concentration but self-
hypnotism. When you fix the eye on a bright
disc you "go off" eventually. Even were you to

close your eyes and focus attention on a single thought, you would reduce the area of consciousness and develop what is known as a "dreamy mental state" of which a good example is the ecstasy of the mystic. Ecstasy, whatever else it is, can be no more than a species of self-hypnotism. The kind of concentration we are dealing with in this lesson has nothing mystical about it. It involves the synthetic working of the whole mind, directed to one end, and all its movements are controlled by the will.

## SELF-CONTROL

The practical effect of this teaching ought to be highly encouraging, for we have met with hundreds of men and women who have wrongly accused themselves of lack of concentration. They had been trying to *fix* their attention on one thing, and because they had failed they became exceedingly depressed. What they lacked was the *control* to order their thoughts and restrict them to a certain, specific path. Too frequently, their attention wandered off aimlessly. Below are reprinted two specimen letters from persons afflicted with this type of mind-wandering:

"The first sentence in a certain magazine article mentions that a prominent fruit merchant has decided to abandon his fruit-growing activities in Florida. I go on to the next sentence, but before I have finished it I have lost the little meaning the first conveyed; for the name Florida brings to mind the 1926 tornado which caused such immense damage and suffering. During the time that my eye is conning the printed symbols of sentence after sentence, my attention flits from tornadoes to fruits, to Florida, to land, to business failure. At last I have to turn back and read the whole page again, much to my disgust. The only kind of book I can read without mind-wandering is a novel with an interesting plot in it."

Here is another letter:

"What does a fellow have to do who cannot settle down to anything for more than five minutes at a time? That's my complaint. I resolve to work at my math, but as soon as I open my books, attention is distracted to something else, and I begin to trace figures or scrawl letters of the alphabet on the paper intended for notes. If you can prescribe some remedy which will prevent my wandering, I will be grateful."

Examine these two cases. They are both alike in that both individuals lack control: the mind of the first man is at the complete mercy of association; that of the second man is a prey to the mood and fancy of the moment. The first person makes some semblance of effort to guide his stream of consciousness; the second ships his oars and drifts with the stream.

## II—CAUSES OF MIND-WANDERING

What are the causes of these conditions? They may be classified as follows:

*Physical causes,* due to nervous illness of various kinds; the effects of shock or accident; excitable temperament; restlessness.

*Mental causes,* due to a profusion of interests; a mind that works very rapidly; natural indolence; lack of interest; the habit of drifting.

*Economic causes,* due to a monotony of daily work; highly specialized duties narrowing the mental sphere.

### SOME CAUSES ANALYZED

This is not a complete list, but it embodies the majority of causes. Take one from each section and study it. The love of excitement, for instance, is a frequent obstacle to concentration. There seems to be a tendency to throw off self-restraint and to yield to sudden impulses, and this tendency we may attribute to the ever-increasing pressure of modern life.

This propensity is fostered in the schools of today, where each lesson is much shorter in duration than was the case a century ago, and every effort is made to render the subjects as pleasant as possible to the student. Although there are undoubtedly arguments in favor of this practice, it is clear that it must operate prejudicially to concentration, for the youthful mind is not

trained, as it formerly was, to devote its con-
tinued attention to matters not inherently pleas-
ing to it.  As a natural result, the emotions of
pleasure or of dislike are constantly being
emphasized.

Huxley has said that "perhaps the most valu-
able result of all education is the ability to make
yourself do the thing you have to do when it has
to be done, *whether you like it or not*.  It is the
first lesson which ought to be learned, and however early a man's training begins, it is probably the last he learns thoroughly."

*Too Many "Interests"*—In the second place,
mind-wandering may be brought about by a profusion of interests.  Here we have a case of too
many irons in the fire.  Many Pelman students
glory in this fact.  They joyfully assert that they
are interested in business, in art, in church work,
in old china, in tennis, in chess, and many other
things, but they usually conclude their letter by
saying: "Somehow or other it seems impossible
to *focus* the mind on anything."  Small wonder!
They have been distributing their attention over
a very wide area; their mind must continually
hop, skip, and jump from one thing to another.

Our capacity for versatility is not unlimited,
and we must not attempt to enlarge it except in
proportion as the power of attention is brought
habitually under control.  If you can attend only
to a few subjects and wish to do well in them, a
radical change in method is necessary.  You must

restrict your range of activities and intensify your focus.

*Monotony of Work*—Among economic causes of mind-wandering none is more potent than the monotony induced by labor that is accomplished automatically. The mind has a tendency to wander at will, but at the same time it does not completely forget the task before it. At certain periods, it returns to adjust an error, to tighten a screw, or to notch a gauge. But it is soon off again, and a year or two of this kind of mental life, *no effort having been made to correct the habit in leisure hours*, makes concentration exercises rather difficult at first. Unless a student has already trained his power, he will be disposed to sidetrack these exercises. That would be folly. Once having undertaken this course of training, persevere as seriously as you have been doing up to this point. Aim at mastery because it will arouse in you a certain self-respect, and because mastery will prove a worthy ideal as well as a real advantage.

## TRACE YOUR OWN CAUSE

If you suffer from mind-wandering, it is of great importance to know what is the cause of it. Should it be traced to a nervous breakdown, you cannot afford to put too much pressure on yourself at first; you must go slowly and be content with steady progress. Should it be traceable to indolence, or to a wrong method of schooling, you can then follow a more Spartan régime; in fact, it is your duty to do so. Instead of alternating concentration and rest, gradually extending the time for concentration by five minutes to thirty minutes in each hour, time yourself for thirty minutes at once, and resolve to see the thing through, however often you fail during your first attempts.

*"Quick" Intellects*—The impetuous and rapid-working mind is another that is frequently encountered. The mental processes of people with such minds move with a speed that is abnormal. They never "continue in one stay," and can seldom concentrate in the ordinary sense. These persons try to amend for the defect by paying *very close attention for brief periods*, like a searchlight, which is focussed here and there, and yet is always "on the move." Some people seem to succeed in this method, and Professor William James, speaking of such men and women, says:

"Some of the most efficient workers I know are of the ultra-scatter-brained type. One friend who does a prodigious quantity of work has in fact confessed to me that, if he wants to get ideas of any subject, he sits down to work at something else, his best results coming through his mind-wanderings. This is perhaps an epigrammatic exaggeration on his part; but I think seriously that no one of us need be too much distressed at his own short-comings in this regard. Our mind may enjoy but little comfort, may be restless and feel confused, but it may be extremely efficient all the time."

We are bound to admit the type is not very plentiful, and no student should plume himself on belonging to this unusual group.

*Does Genius "Mind-Wander?"*—But the type does exist, although specimens are few and far between. The late Professor Jules Henri Poincaré, famous physicist and mathematician, is said to have been one. His mental methods were closely analyzed by an expert, and the verdict was pronounced that the famous mathematician's power of abstraction could only be described as flighty, unstable and uncontrolled. He seemed to possess those very qualities which might have made him a great novelist, instead of the great student of science and mathematics.

On the other hand, Poincaré himself, in his *Science and Method*, says that he often spent a whole evening solving a problem. When one has spent as many hours of really close concentration as Poincaré, it can hardly be said that the person's powers of concentration are spasmodic, uncontrolled, and unstable.

What Poincaré did believe in most strongly was to alternate between concentration for a period and other work or recreation, the idea being that an unsolved problem would be solved in the subconscious sphere during the interval, and would, later on, announce the solution to the conscious mind. Still, men of genius are not proper models for the majority of people, especially when testimony as to the methods of the geniuses is conflicting. As far as most of us are concerned, close attention is the only way to achieve any possible results.

*About Intuitions*—There is also another type which is much more common, represented by those men who never seem to *ponder* their problems at all. They arrive at a solution at once, though they acted intuitively. How are such cases explained? There are two possible answers: First, such decisions usually concern a man's business or profession, or something with which long experience has made him familiar. Secondly, these decisions are excellent examples of psycho-synthesis where mental functions, like reasoning, memory and imagination, do not work in semi-separation, but unitedly, as a whole. It is the ideal method, but is attainable only when one gives each function its appropriate training in accordance with the principles laid down in these lessons.

## III—THE ADVANTAGES OF CONCENTRATION

It may seem hardly necessary to expound further on the importance of the power of concentration, but we propose to do so in order that the reader may grasp the salient facts more firmly.

## DEVELOPMENT OF MENTAL FUNCTIONS

The first and most obvious advantage of controlled attention is that the whole of the mental functions are thereby developed to the limit of their capacity. The act of close attention means that, in the act of examining an object, or an idea, you are unconsciously exercising your memory, recalling similar objects or ideas. You are using your imagination in conceiving improvement by change. You are all the time comparing and contrasting, testing theories and accepting or rejecting them.

Concentrate on a new "make" of automobile, for example, or on anything about which you have some knowledge already, and you will find all these mental processes at work, as a reconstruction of your thinking will show. There is no merit in concentration itself; its value lies in the opportunity it affords for the functioning of our mental powers as a whole. There is no illumination in it *per se;* even a searchlight cannot throw its beams into the sky without the help of the mechanism which makes light and focus possible, and this mechanism does for the searchlight precisely what concentration does for the mind.

*It Brings Accurate Knowledge*—The second advantage of controlled attention is that it brings accurate knowledge. One can see many things, without *really* seeing them. We sense them,

but do not know them; or we think so super-
ficially about an idea that it always remains
vague to us.   Until we give real attention to a
phenomenon we cannot truly know it, even
though the phenomenon be no more than the pen
with which we write, or the ink that flows from
it.

## OBSERVANT ATTENTION

Hallock tells us that a teacher once said to
the pupils of a large school, all of whom had
often seen cows: " 'I should like to find out how
many of you know whether a cow's ears are
above, below, behind, or in front of her horns.
I want only those pupils to raise their hands who
are sure they know and who will promise to give
a dollar to charity if the answer is wrong.' Only
two hands were raised.   Their owners had *drawn*
the cows, and in order to do so had been forced
to concentrate their attention upon the animals.

"Fifteen pupils were sure that they had seen
cats climb trees and descend them.   There was
unanimity of opinion that the cats went up head
first.   When asked whether the cats came down
head or tail first, the majority were sure that the
cats had descended as they were never known
to do.   Anyone who had ever noticed the shape
of the claws of any beast of prey could have answered that question without having witnessed
an actual descent.

"Farmers' boys, who have often seen cows
and horses lie down and rise, are seldom sure

whether the animals rise with their fore or hind legs first, or whether the movements of the horse in rising are similar to those of the cow. The elm leaf has a certain peculiarity which is discernable at first glance, yet only about five per cent. of the pupils of a certain school incorporated this peculiarity in their drawing. Perception, to achieve satisfactory results, must summon the will to its aid to concentrate attention. Only the smallest part of what falls upon our senses at any time is actually perceived."

*Lawyers' Agreements*—The reading of a lawyer's agreement is too often done perfunctorily; sometimes in a spirit of trustfulness, sometimes because a busy hour is unfortunately selected for the purpose, and sometimes because time is short and signatures are awaited. But later, when trouble begins and the agreement must be consulted, one pays the penalty for having given diffuse and meager attention. That client always suffers who cannot concentrate and proceeds on the assumption that all clauses have been included in the contract.

## THE MIND OF THE EXPERT

All the way through life, this want of attention exacts its penalties. Many of us began life lacking training in attention, and we have industriously followed a false start. A happy distinction from this type of mind is furnished by the mind of the expert.

An expert is one who has become a master in discrimination: he can diagnose new circumstances because he is proficient in his knowledge of similarities and differences in connection with his subject; and his mastery is the direct outcome of his concentration.

If he is skilled in woodcraft he knows the trees by their outlines, even in winter. If he is a keen musician he can point out the differences between two or more renderings of a pianoforte sonata, subtle differences which would have escaped the untrained ear. If he is a man of science he can value a new hpyothesis in a convincing manner, because his past training has taught him the significance of minutiæ as well as given him the ability to detect the difference between what is only apparent and what is real.

*Aim at Mastery*—It is cheering to know that most of us can be experts in *something* and that the secret of it lies in developing the simple habit of close attention. To be a master in one sphere of knowledge, however humble, is to engender a kind of intellectual self-respect; not egotism or vanity, not foolish pride or unpleasant self-assertion, but a feeling that in some way we have justified the existence of our intelligence by causing it to serve an ideal. Keep this ideal of mastery before you and you will find that the habit of concentration is easily formed.

*Increases Memory Power*—The third advantage of controlled attention is that impressions are more securely retained. We forget a good deal because we never really knew what we now desire to recall. The first impression of the fact, the idea, or the person, was sketchy; it was neither definite nor vivid; we had not aimed at mastery or accuracy. It may be taken as a good general rule that *attention means memory*. You cannot recall what you have never known. If the original experience is vague, the result of the attempt to recall it will be vague also.

Here again we meet with the ethical element in mental training: you reap only that which you have sown. If you sow carelessness you cannot expect to reap accuracy. If you sow inattention you must not look for a rich harvest of recollections. If you sow indifference to life, you cannot hope to reap the fruits of a fine sensibility.

To get the best of what the world offers, its outward benefits as well as its inward experiences, one must put some conscience into living; and this necessity is nowhere more manifest, in its intellectual associations, than in the way in which the valued stores of memory are dependent on the conscientious discharge of the duty of attention. *Your memory power is largely in your own hands.* You can make it what you will. Wandering will result in a mass of vague and unorganized data; concentration, in an organized, classified and easily recognizable unit.

## CONCENTRATION AND ORIGINALITY

The fourth advantage of controlled attention is the aid which it gives to discovery and originality. New ideas are often unexpected and unbidden, from which fact one must not infer that ideas are only inspirations, and the creation of them is completely beyond our control. This is not so. No man conceives many brilliant or original ideas in matters to which he has given little thought, or in those of which he is wholly ignorant.

If Marshal Foch received an inspiration on the battlefield, an idea which ultimately opened up a new aspect of warfare, it was because he was thoroughly versed in strategy and tactics. The garbage man is often a valued member of the community, but we do not expect him to show originality in painting, or political economy. We do expect him, however, to have an open mind for new ideas on cans with dog-defying lids. Indeed he is more likely to have ideas on that subject than anybody else, unless it be the manufacturers.

*The Mark of Great Minds*—It is a commonplace in psychology that one of the chief differences between a mind of great calibre and one of less is this very power of concentrated attention. Men, like Sir Isaac Newton, whose names are associated with distinctively original conceptions, have displayed remarkable ability for forgetting for hours at a time, the immediate concerns of the world and for devoting their whole attention to some problem calling for solution.

Sir William Hamilton has said that "the difference between an ordinary mind and the mind of Newton consists principally in this, that one is capable of the application of a more continuous attention than the other; that a Newton is able without fatigue, to connect inference with inference in one long series towards a determined end; while the man of inferior capability is soon obliged to break or let fall the thread which he had begun to spin . . . To one who complimented him on his genius Newton replied, that if he had made any discoveries, it was owing more to patient attention than to any other talent."[1]

## THE REQUIRED PREPARATORY WORK

This does not mean that *any* man by concentrating long enough could have made the same discoveries, or that by *merely* focussing his attention on his own affairs an engineer will suddenly see, as in a vision, the outline of an entirely new machine. *There is a preparatory condition.* In Newton's case it was a sense of profound wonder in the presence of Nature, a deep knowledge of physical force, and a consuming desire to discover the secrets of the heavens.

In the case of James Watt it was a close fam-

---

[1] *Lectures on Metaphysics*, Vol. I, p. 256.

iliarity with mathematics and with the mechanics
of water engines which formed the basis of his
discoveries in steam-power. This acquaintance
afforded the raw material for the new meditation
which the presence of Newcomen's water-lifting
engine stimulated within him. Both Newton and
Watt possessed that absorbing interest-power
which is really the primary agent in producing
new ideas.

Concentration gives the creative impulse its
full opportunity. This opportunity may not be
fruitful during the period of concentration, or
indeed during several periods; for experience
shows that the new idea will often come suddenly and unexpectedly, perhaps when the mind
is occupied with an altogether different matter.
But it is also true that those new ideas seldom
come unless a certain amount of close attention
has preceded them. In every genesis creation
and order follows confusion and chaos.

## RELATIVITY OF INTEREST

While it would be ideal to have one engaged
in work which is naturally attractive, it must be
admitted that even under the most fortunate
conditions a man is frequently called upon to
concentrate his attention on matters which are
not congenial to his mood. In such cases it is use-
less to wait for the distaste to pass away. Often
it is not practicable to do so. Circumstances may
not permit of delay; moreover, the distaste may

grow rather than diminish. But if it is impossible to concentrate for any considerable time on a matter in which one is not interested, what is one to do? It looks like an *impasse*. It is not an *impasse*, however. Let us be quite clear as to the meaning of this word Interest.

Interest does not, although we commonly speak as if it did, stand for a quality inherent in the object. Nothing is interesting in an absolute sense. Everything is interesting only in a relative sense—that is to say, in relation to a given individual. This fundamental fact, therefore, indicates a certain *attitude of mind;* and the mind is capable in this matter of adjustment within a very wide range. It is here that Will plays its part, based on the interplay of Thought (or judgment) and Feeling. Will gives the initial impulse in a certain direction, overbears the primary opposition. Once having done this, it enables one to resist the solicitations that are apt to throng upon one from other quarters. It serves as a sentry to keep out intruders: it scotches irrelevant ideas the moment they intrude their uninvited faces above the threshold of consciousness. After a while, with practice and discipline, a man may depend upon himself to find interest even in the most unpromising material, and thus to maintain his attention in perfect focus.

Some of our students may find it interesting to pursue this question of Interest a little further.

Why, for instance, of two students of equal ability who have undergone similar courses of training, will one find it easy to apply himself conscientiously to Mathematics and loathe Anatomy, while the other will be enthusiastic about Anatomy and find Mathematics repulsive? The reason for the difference is bound up in the whole mass of previous experience of the one and the other.

We may consider the mind as consisting of a number of masses of co-ordinated knowledge tinged with emotion: a number of "complexes," to use a word which has been chosen by some psychologists. Such complexes have grown from a small nucleus by the absorption of ideas which they are capable of building up into their substance. The larger they have grown the greater has become their power of assimilation and the more greedy are they for new food.

In a highly specialized mind, some particular complex has come to dominate the whole personality: law, we may suppose, if you are a lawyer; philosophy and theology, if you are a clergyman; medicine, if you are a physician. Each comprises many minor complexes, and the whole structure soon becomes a very elaborate affair. Against its power of self-assertion, if it is necessary to foster a minor complex, the will comes into play for the protection of the latter against its powerful rivals; will, which may indeed be counted a thing in itself, but which, in its particular direction, is the resultant of the mental forces that we segregate under the headings of Thought and Feeling. As, under its shelter, knowledge increases, so interest (that is to say, a readiness to attend to a particular matter) increases also.

Resistance tends constantly to diminish as the new complex grows stronger by comparison with those that have already been well-established, with the result that, given sufficient motive either of self-interest or of some other instinctive urge, the anatomist becomes in addition a mathematician, and the mathematician a master of anatomy. Upon this aspect of the matter we would lay special stress for the encouragement of students who are constrained by force of circumstances to devote their lives to some form of activity not altogether of their own choosing.

## IV—THE MORALS OF CONCENTRATION

The mind of man is an arena in which is being constantly fought a moral conflict, and it is upon this conception that the principle explained in the preceding paragraphs has been based. The function of the psychologist is to show us how to displace the less desirable thoughts by concentrating on the more desirable. As mental control is thus established, so the plague of unwholesome ideas comes to an end; we have overcome evil with good; and we have become so deeply interested in the right thing, or the thing that is useful, that the other never gets a chance.

Thus, if we are not directly and immediately responsible for the thoughts that enter our minds, we must at any rate answer for those that we allow to remain there. Yet, in a certain sense, we *are* responsible for at least some of our involuntary thoughts, as was shown in an earlier lesson, where we did a little exploration of the region of the Subconscious.

## V—HOW TO DEVELOP CONCENTRATION

Turn back to Lesson III. In that Lesson we pointed out the great importance of *Interest*, and we anticipated the general course of our present remarks. Active attention springs, as a rule from interest; that is, the emotional element is the compelling power. But there is also (as we have shown) an interest which is the off-spring of attention.

There are many middle-aged men who have *acquired* a liking for golf. At first they had no interest in the game, and laboriously traversed the links as a matter of course. But, slowly interest began to grow, and as it grew attention to the game demanded less effort. Later, this middle-aged person who grumblingly, and often angrily, had walked after the little white ball, became an ardent golfer. Although in the first place attention had created interest, it was interest now which sustained attention. It may be stated as a law that *voluntary attention* (i.e., attention depending upon an impulse of the will), *tends eventually to give place to spontaneous attention.*

## GENERAL CONDITIONS OF SUCCESS

Apart from interest, however, there are certain other conditions on which concentration depends for its success. The most important of these are:

(a) The proper physical and mental states.

(b) The practice of exercises on approved lines.

(c) The transformation of effort into habit. This habit is the ultimate aim of all training. Concentration should be so natural that there will be a trivial expenditure of effort in applying oneself to any object or idea which calls for attention.

*Physical Conditions*—Ideal conditions imply that the body and brain are without pain or fatigue; that the bodily position is free from discomfort, and that the atmosphere is hygienic. There should be no distraction of elements like continuous and irritating noises. It may be said that one cannot always have control over such conditions. That is true. But the majority of men and women can secure most of them; and as far as they cannot do so, all can learn to adapt themselves to the actual conditions of their lives.

Livingstone tells us that he did all his early studying amid the roar of a factory. Journalists, especially, often acquire the ability to concentrate anywhere.

*Concentration and Digestion*—Many people attempt to concentrate upon difficult mental work immediately after a meal. This is a time which should better be given up to light reading or to mental work that is more or less mechanical. The digestive processes are interrupted when the meal is followed by intensive thought. Open-air exercise of a non-strenuous nature, or some kind of social recreation, is often the best way of resting and adjusting bodily and mental conditions after a meal.

*Mental Conditions*—Given proper physical conditions, the mental conditions are bound to have a good start. But we must not lay too great dependence on this start. A bit of bad news may break in upon our otherwise satisfactory effort, and the whole mind may become incapable of further prolonged attention. There are other factors also at work, and to some of the more important of them we shall now direct your attention. There is the mistake of trying to *force* concentration upon a mind already tired. By offering something of interest, one may possibly *tempt* or *induce* a tired mind into a state of close attention, but it is not wise to do so if the time for rest has arrived. Exhaustion of energy should be followed by a period of repair.

As already explained, the underlying intention of every exercise and of all formal discipline is to develop habit and facility, so that we may be able to do almost unconsciously what before required much conscious effort. A beginner with the violin uses finger exercises to give him mastery over technique. At first he "feels" for his notes; afterwards he finds them automatically. The same principle may be applied to mental exercises. We practice in order that concentration shall not be a conscious and formal effort, but rather a habit of arousing interest in whatever may be the enterprise of the moment.

## EASE AND ECONOMY

The ideal condition is so to obtain the control of thought as to be able to turn our attention in any direction we desire, and in this way we accomplish a true *economy of action*. If, when engaged in conversation, we had to think of the technical rules governing each expression, we would ourselves be exhausted at the end of a half-hour's talk. But because we have mastered the rules of grammar we obey them unconsciously, and can devote our whole attention to the precise formulation of the ideas we wish to express. It would mean great economy to automatize mental control; for the purpose of achieving this economy every student should try to increase the number of mental powers that may be relied upon to act spontaneously.

He should so train his abilities that he will perceive, remember, concentrate, imagine, and resolve without any seeming effort. This is the condition referred to by Professor Whitehead in his *Introduction to Mathematics*. After explaining some figures he says: "This example shows that, by the aid of symbolism, we can make transitions in reasoning, almost mechanically by the eye, which would otherwise call into play the higher faculties of the brain. It is a truism, repeated by all copybooks and by eminent people that we should cultivate the habit of thinking of what we are doing. The precise opposite is the case. Civilization advances by extending the number of important operations which we can perform without thinking about them." It is this service that PELMANISM accomplishes for all its serious students.

At first, we *are* and we *must* be conscious of what we are doing. In a general sense it must always be so, but there are numerous spheres of activity where growth depends on this ability to do unconsciously what we used to do consciously. As Titchener has it, "the more a piece of work is reduced to a matter of course, the more power has the mind to advance to further work."[1]

*The "Least Effort" in Observation*—The man who has worked our exercises thoroughly never thinks about the exercises themselves; he sees, and notices, and thinks simultaneously; and

---

[1] *Primer of Psychology*, p. 87.

he does these things with much greater efficiency than ever before. He has no need to say, when he rises in the morning, "I must keep my eyes and ears open today." He used to do that once—when he was a learner; but when reflective observation became a habit, he began, quite unconsciously, to observe men and things with a keenness hitherto unknown. The same principle applies to his thought forces. Previously, he floundered about, wondering what next would be best to "take up"; or else he never wondered at all. Then one day an idea came to him which he thought was worthwhile. He nurtured that idea until he began to see in it great possibilities of profit. Today he is hard at work trying to embody his dream in action; but he seldom expresses it in words, even to himself. Ambition has become a habit with him; he moves because he must. A similar story may be told of this man's memory. He toiled with exercises and methods for a long period, until the training began to have its natural, depressing effect. But now recollection, which once demanded a mighty effort, is almost a lightning process, because attention and concentration are ready servants of his Will, yielding a kind of knowledge that is vivid and permanent.

You see now what is meant by economy of effort. Every added ability facilitates work because the habitualization of certain acts permits more scope for the exercise of higher functions.

*Apply this Lesson*—If your power of concentration is not what it ought to be, *search for the cause of the trouble.* You will soon find it. As often as not, the root of the difficulty lies in a previously formed *bad habit.* The first thing to do is to set to work to establish the right habit. Success depends on understanding the nature of concentration, as explained in the preceding pages, and on persistent practice of the exercises. If you resolve to be master of your mental processes, you *will* be master. Regard this matter seriously. The time and trouble thus spent, regarded as an investment, will pay you dividends of incalculable value. To show how practical such mental exercises can be made, study the following section.

## THE SECRET OF ORGANIZATION

There are two chief questions before every Organizer:

1. What is the work to be done, or the aim to be achieved?

2. What is the best way of accomplishing it?

Out of these two questions many others will arise; and when these have been answered, temporarily or finally, the practical part of the scheme can be set in motion.

Let us suppose that the task to be performed is the arrangement of a local concert, and that the task of taking charge devolves upon someone who has had no experience in such enterprises. Under the first question fall the items of hiring a hall, engaging artists, the printing of bills, programs and tickets, and a score of others. Question 2 needs to be applied to every one of these separate considerations.

There is a right method of selecting artists, and a wrong one; one can pay as much for poor artists who have no power of filling the house as for others whose names will crowd it; there is a properly varied program, and one that is spoiled by its monotony. Success in such an enterprise calls for the use of the imagination; and even when imagination in the selection of speakers or performers has been exercised, often the person in charge may realize too late that he has neglected to discharge a certain fundamental duty. For instance, he may have forgotten to select a concert hall of sufficient capacity.

Everyone has to organize *something*, his personal expenditure, moving from one house to another, the furthering of his business, the extension of his clientele, or preparation for an examination. Let us have done with all slipshod methods. We are now the disciples of system, and system is method applied to life's affairs. For the sake of practice, choose a subject from the list below as a home exercise in concentration and imagination, as well as in organization.

On paper briefly outline how you would solve the problem which you select.

1. The formation of a Literary Society.
2. Applying for a position.
3. Fitting out a boy for a boarding-school.
4. A house-to-house political canvassing scheme.
5. Writing a book on Salesmanship.
6. Arranging a railway excursion.

## VI—DON'TS

1. Don't try to *screw down* your powers of attention.

2. Don't chastise yourself if at first, despite everything, you fail to concentrate. Resolve to see the thing through.

3. Don't forget to analyze the *causes* of your mind-wandering. To know them is halfway to success.

4. Don't be superficial. Get at the fundamentals.

5. When reading, don't abandon a sentence until you are positive that you have grasped every idea contained in it.

6. Don't forget that Concentration is, after all, a *habit*, and that practice is consequently essential.

## VII—THIS DO

1. Form the ideal: "I will concentrate whenever I wish to do so."

2. Make the attainment of this ideal a matter of *conscience* and *self-respect*.

3. Remember that the adage about "too many irons in the fire" is still true.

4. Become an expert in *something*, however ordinary it may appear to be.

5. If concentrative efforts fail, analyze the *conditions*.

6. Aim at ease in concentration. It saves time and energy.

# VIII—MENTAL EXERCISES

## EXERCISE XXVI

Take a pencil and sheet of paper. From the newspaper select a subject that offers some scope for argument; for example, an editorial on the rapid strides made in the field of aeronautics during the last few years. The thought occurs to you: will the development of the airplane take place in as short a period of time as did that of the automobile?

Write down your thoughts just as they come; never mind their lack of sequence. Your present aim is to concentrate on one subject for at least a quarter of an hour; only by writing continuously will you be likely to succeed in concentrating.

If you feel you must answer a question that arises, by all means do so. Perhaps you will write for twenty minutes or half an hour, without allowing your attention to wander for a moment. Thus the exercise will justify itself. The accuracy of your questions and answers is not unimportant, but it is quite secondary in this connection. Your aim is not to discuss literature, journalism, or philosophy, but to afford yourself practice in mind-training. Such an exercise should be practiced until the student feels he can do it easily. There ought to be no difficulty in finding subjects in the current periodicals. Here are some suggestions:

(a) The educational value of the cinema.
(b) Companionate marriage.
(c) What is the matter with education?
(d) What kind of books shall we read?
(e) An aerial Atlantic service.
(f) The League of Nations.
(g) Laws that ought to be abolished.
(h) Capital Punishment.
(i) Have we seen the last war?

## EXERCISE XXVII

It would be preferable to select a subject that is not particularly attractive, and concentrate upon it by trying to follow its arguments as set out by the writer whose words you propose to study.

When you have made your choice, concentrate upon it at first for ten minutes, then increase the time by five minutes until you can attend to it for half an hour easily. You had better use the pencil and paper methods, as before, asking questions and writing answers. Or you may write an analysis. The aim, of course, is not *knowledge*, but *control* of mental operations, the value of which control we have already discussed. We are told that to make an uninteresting subject interesting, by paying attention to it, is better training for the mind than paying attention to an interesting subject. It is *good* training, but not better. The Spartan was a worshipper of discipline for discipline's sake;

but it was not the Spartan Greeks who led the world.

Nevertheless, no Pelman student can afford to neglect anything that is *good* training. Practice this exercise until you can do it easily. Such subjects as Bimetallism, the game laws, and currency problems are generally voted unattractive by the majority of people. It may be an excess of Spartan discipline to follow the late Dr. Martineau, who when a young man compelled himself to devote his best energies to the subjects for which he had no aptitude or liking. A little discipline of this kind is good for all of us.

### EXERCISE XXVIII

Paraphrasing is the art of recasting thought in the common language of the day. We paraphrase for the purpose of making the meaning clearer and richer. The value of paraphrasing is manifold. It is not only an exercise in concentration, but it affords one excellent practice in exact thinking and proper use of words. Paraphrasing will help you to make use of your vocabulary and also to increase it.

Let us choose a simple proverb like: He who would eat the kernel must crack the nut.

Rewritten it might be rendered: Those who would reap rewards must work for them. Again it might be expressed: We must work for what we get.

Always be sure to retain the original meaning. You may expand or enlarge the thought but must not introduce a new thought or one that is irrevelant.

Below are some proverbs which will give you opportunity for practice in paraphrasing, and incidentally interpreting and thinking:

1. Make hay while the sun shines.
2. A stitch in time saves nine.
3. In a calm sea every man is a pilot.
4. A drowning man will grasp at a straw.
5. Rats desert a sinking ship.
6. It takes more than one swallow to make a summer.
7. Every rose has its thorn.
8. A tree is known by its fruit.
9. No wind can do him good who steers for no port.
10. The crab tree planted where one wills will never bear sweet apples.

Develop your ability in this type of exercise by paraphrasing, orally, sentences from books or from newspaper leading articles.

It is not to be supposed that you will always be able to improve upon the original. In the case of a passage taken from a classic you will hardly expect to be able to do so. But the effort will fix your attention; it will build up the analytical habit upon which clear thinking depends; and, finally, by exercising your vocabulary, it will improve your powers of self-expression.

# IX—HEALTH EXERCISES

## EIGHTH LESSON

"A lean horse for a fast race" is a very familiar saying and has considerable truth in it. There can be no question that those who are slender are more active than the so-called fat persons, and still the former are prone to burn up a much greater amount of energy than the latter. Nobody wants to be "skinny" nor do many people care to be corpulent. Inasmuch as neither condition is ideal, it becomes a question of just how these conditions can be prevented. Neither a very thin, nor a very stout person can hope to be happy if he attempts to reduce or gain weight after he has reached middle age. The only profitable time to essay gaining or losing weight is during the period of youth, while the body is still responsive to change. There are many exceptions to this statement but for one of middle age to attempt alteration of any kind would be not only a gamble but folly. That person would do better to try a simple remedy, one that has for its purpose the preparation of the body to meet its daily demands with the least expenditure of energy or vitality. It is peculiar of any exercise that it can reduce weight and also build weight up. The first process is destructive, the second is constructive. The exercises described in these lessons are not intended, primarily, to bring about

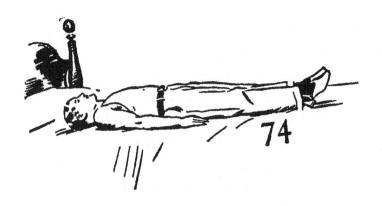

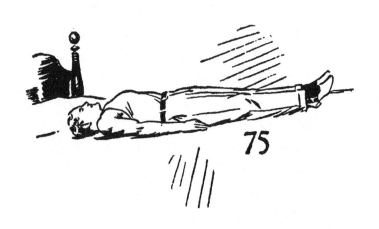

reduction but they will, if performed consistently and faithfully, give the flesh and muscle the elastic tone of normal tissue.

Weight most often accumulates about the abdomen. The various stretching exercises which have been described help this condition in a general way, but we will from now on occupy ourselves with new forms of movement that are particularly planned to reduce the abdominal region.

## WATER WAVE

While still in bed, stretch out full length, and without inhaling raise the chest as far up toward the chin as you can (Fig. 75). To do this, flatten your abdomen (stomach) as much as possible. Now lower the chest by pushing the abdomen down toward your hips as far as you can comfortably push it (Fig. 74). This position will resemble waves of water rolling back and forth in a tub. You should breathe in as normally as permissible, when the chest is raised, and breathe out when you raise the abdomen. Twenty times for each movement will be enough for a beginning.

## STRAIGHT LEG WALK

Now try the Rolling exercise while still in bed. Then, when you get up, stretch your arms high over your head, raise yourself on tip-toes and walk about thirty steps in this position with the knees straight. Don't let your chin sink forward onto your chest. Stand straight and walk straight. To warm up try twenty counts of the Windmill and then face your chair. Stand about four inches from the chair and place both hands (palms) on the forward half of the seat. Keep your arms straight and, keeping feet together, step back about four foot lengths from the chair. Your hands are still on the chair and your body is in a bent position, both heels on the floor (Fig. 76).

## PRONE LEAN

Now sway forward until your head touches the back of the chair, or until your body has straightened out. You will have to rock forward on your toes but do not bend your arms (Fig. 77). Ten times to begin with will be enough.

78

79

## CHARGING

Stand with your feet together and then place your right foot about thirty inches straight to your right. Toes pointing to the right, bend your right knee and keep your left leg straight with foot flat on the floor. Your body is vertically straight and only the right leg has moved. Now place your finger-tips together behind your neck, elbows back, chest high and chin up (Fig. 78). Bend as far to your left as comfort will permit, trying not to alter your body position in any other direction (Fig. 79). There should be a very perceptible strain on your right side. Straighten the right leg, bend the left knee and let your body sway over toward the right. This movement resembles the Tree Swaying, except that here we are using a leg combination to make the exercise slightly more difficult. Ten times on each side will prove adequate.

80

## PUNT

Nearly everybody has witnessed a football game and seen the ball kicked high and far for forty, fifty or more yards. We will take the Football Punt for our natural exercise.

In our previous lesson we practice high kicking, so that Punting should come easy, as the movement is very similar. Stand with feet spread apart about ten inches, body upright and hands out at shoulder level, palms facing one another before you. You are catching the ball: holding it at shoulder height, take a step diagonally to the right in front of the right foot with the left foot. The step should be about two feet long. The hands are still held high. Now slightly lower the hands as if dropping the ball and at the same time kick toward your hands with the right foot (Fig. 80). Point your toes and keep the knee straight. The hands naturally go high over the head, the body is barely tilted backward. The weight of the body is high on the toes of the left foot. A good punter always finishes with his foot higher than his head. Recover by bringing the right foot to the floor. Repeat on the left side. Five times for each should be enough.

## SCOTCH DANCE No. 2

Now, to give ourselves a rapid drill, we will try another Scotch Dance Step.

Hold hands on your hips, the back of the hands resting just over your hip bones.

(1) Hop on your left foot and touch the toes of your right foot to the floor straight out toward your right (Fig. 81).

(2) Hop again on your left foot and cross your right foot over in front of your left knee; the right heel is about knee high, the toes are pointed down and the right knee faces the side (Fig. 82).

(3) Hop again on the left foot and swing the right foot toward the right around behind the left knee, the right knee still out to the right (Fig. 83).

(4) Hop once more on the left foot and return the right foot, locking the front of the left knee. (1) Now jump onto the right and touch the left foot to the floor. (2) Hop on the right and cross the left in front of the right as before. (3) Hop on the right and swing the left behind. (4) Hop on the right and bring the left in front. (1) Repeat on left. Sixteen counts on left. Sixteen counts on right.

## SUGGESTIONS

Some people feel that meals consisting of bread, vegetable and meat furnish a perfectly balanced diet. In a general sense this is true, but in the long run, it turns out to be a very unsatisfactory policy. Variety is essential to any well ordered plan of dietetics. Perhaps the most ignored form of easily assimilated food is fruit. Apples, oranges, figs, dates, bananas, raisins, etc., which are always handy, should be part of everyone's daily diet. Make it a practice to eat some fruit at least once a day. Raw fruits are better than cooked fruits and can always be kept conveniently at hand.

*Reference:*

    STAND STRAIGHT. (DOOR TOPS)
    ROLLING.
    TREE SWAYING.
    ROWING.
    SCOTCH DANCE No. 1.

# SPECIAL INSTRUCTIONS AS TO PROGRESS SHEETS AND TEXT BOOKS

1. Write your name and address legibly on every Progress Sheet.
2. Your number should appear on all your communications; otherwise much unnecessary labor will devolve on the staff.
3. Do not think that your answer must be confined always to the space beneath the question; use additional sheets if you desire.
4. The Text Books should be kept by the student for future reference. Remember you will want to use these attractive and durably bound books for years to come. They will be a library of practical value for you.
5. From seven to ten days are usually sufficient for the mastery of a Text Book and the completion of the Progress Sheet, but it is possible to finish in a briefer period. Everything depends on the student's leisure. There is no fixed time for the return of Progress Sheets

# Recommended Readings

- The Anatomy of Success, Nicolas Darvas

- The Dale Carnegie Course on Effective Speaking, Personality Development, and the Art of How to Win Friends & Influence People, Dale Carnegie

- The Law of Success In Sixteen Lessons by Napoleon Hill (Complete, Unabridged), Napoleon Hill

- It Works, R. H. Jarrett

- The Art of Public Speaking (Audio CD), Dale Carnegie,

- The Success System That Never Fails (Audio CD), W. Clement Stone

- Three Magic Words: The Key to Power, Peace and Plenty ,Uell Stanley Anderson

- The Power of Your Subconscious Mind, Dr. Joseph Murphy (Audio Book on CD)

- As a Man Thinketh by James Allen (Audio Book on CD) , James Allen

- The Science of Mind, Ernest Holmes

- Dynamic Laws of Prosperity, Catherine Ponder

- Think and Grow Rich, Napoleon Hill

- The Wisdom of Wallace D. Wattles: Including - The Science of Getting Rich,The Science of Being Great & The Science of Being Well , Wallace D. Wattles

- Game of life and how to play it , Florence Scovel

CPSIA information can be obtained at www.ICGtesting.com
Printed in the USA
BVOW08s1227041114

373599BV00022B/719/P